# SEVEN STEPS TO A LIFE OF SIGNIFICANCE

## PAUL R. BROWN

with KEVIN S. PATTERSON
and LESLIE BROWN

## Seven Steps to a Life of Significance

© 2015 Paul R. Brown. All Rights Reserved.
With Kevin S. Patterson & Leslie Brown Scales

Published by SOS Publishing

All rights reserved. The authors and publisher have done their best to give proper credit where credit is due. No part of this book may be reproduced or transmitted in any form or by any means, electronic or mechanical, including photocopying and recording, or by an information storage and retrieval system, without permission in writing from the authors.

ISBN: 978-1-943157-06-8

REACH THE AUTHOR:

www.LeadershipDynamicsInc.com

Printed in the United States of America

## Dedication

What did I ever do in my life to be blessed by the friendship and love of such a special woman?

I dedicate this book to my wife Lois, my human source of inspiration for all that I am and do which is significant to me. Having the privilege to hold your hand through the many ups and downs of our shared journey of life has given me the strength, courage and reason to persevere and ultimately prevail. You are my joie de vivre and true north.

*To Howie –*
*May the ideas in this book inspire you to new levels of significance and success.*

*Best Wishes,*
*Paul*
*May 2017*

## Acknowledgments

Researching, writing and publishing a book is not an individual effort. It is truly a collaboration of experience, knowledge and talent. I have been blessed by the influence, friendship, support and cooperation of many individuals who have made the dream of publishing this book possible.

Many of the individuals who have made this book possible I have never met or known personally. They most likely will never know that their work has influenced me and helped to form me. They are the many authors who have inspired me through their writings and audio programs. I have been a student of their philosophies, interpretations and insights into the basic tenants which have made individuals successful and significant over the last five thousand years. There really aren't any new ideas, there are simply new ways of interpreting and communicating them in different ways which resonate with us individually and facilitate understanding and meaning of important life principles and lessons.

To name all of the authors who have influenced me would take up much of this book. Some of the most significant to me have been Paul J. Meyer, Jim Rohn, Brian Tracey, Dan Sullivan, Napoleon Hill, Earl Nightingale, Rev. Norman Vincent Peale, Dale Carnegie, Rev. Robert Schuller, Denis Waitley, James Allen, M. Scott Peck, Deepak Chopra, Stephen Covey, and Ken Blanchard. I am grateful to all of these individuals for their work and influence on my thinking and formation.

There is another group of individuals who contributed greatly to making this lifetime goal a reality. Without them it would simply have not been possible. Rev. Kevin Patterson has been a major contributor. He has labored tirelessly to ensure the quality of the book's content through his research, writing, editing and moral support. Kevin's scholarly knowledge of literature, grammar, and style has been an invaluable resource. I consider Kevin's collaboration and friendship to be a true blessing in my life.

I would be remiss if I did not thank Kevin's children Julia, Tony and Alex for the many contributions that they have made through the completion of the countless important tasks and minor details which were delegated to them throughout the course of this project. Your enthusiasm and zest for life and all that you do is infectious.

Lastly, I would like to thank my daughter, Leslie Brown Scales, for her hours of proofing, editing, research and coordination of the publishing of this book. It has been a great source of joy and pride to have you involved in this book and my life's work.

# TABLE OF CONTENTS

| | |
|---|---|
| Dedication | 3 |
| Acknowledgments | 4 |
| CHAPTER ONE – SELF-IMAGE: Who are you, really? | 8 |
| CHAPTER TWO – VISION: What is your purpose in life? | 22 |
| CHAPTER THREE – MISSION: How will you fulfill your purpose? | 36 |
| CHAPTER FOUR – LIFE STRATEGIES: How will you accomplish your mission? | 50 |
| CHAPTER FIVE – SETTING GOALS: How will you get from here to there? | 72 |
| CHAPTER SIX – HIGH PAYOFF ACTIVITIES: How can you maximize your effectiveness? | 92 |
| CHAPTER SEVEN – SELF-DISCIPLINE: Do you have what it takes? | 102 |
| Final Thoughts | 127 |
| About the Co-Authors | 137 |
| Footnotes | 139 |

## Chapter One

"Profound joy of the heart is like a magnet that indicates the path of life."
– *Mother Theresa*

# SELF-IMAGE: Who Are You, Really?

## Step #1 Is Knowing Who You Are

**Part I: Your Sources of True Joy**

You are in the middle of your work day, just an ordinary day, and then suddenly it happens... again. In the back of your mind, you hear these nagging questions. What am I doing this for? What does it all mean? Why am I doing this instead of what I really want to do? When do I get to start doing the things I love? How does what I do make a difference? Then your cell phone rings, covering up the noise of the unanswered questions... but they don't go away.

You are facing a crisis of meaning, and it could be the beginning of the most important journey of your life. It was for me. My personal crisis of meaning came at a time when I had achieved success in my career, and went home every night to a wonderful wife and two amazing daughters. At some point, though, I just seemed to stop growing, and lost any sense of making a difference in the world. What's worse, I was missing out on so much that I truly cared about, like time with my family, in order to pursue business goals that no longer brought me joy.

It was about twenty years ago, and I was involved in one of the most difficult decisions of my life. I was trying to decide whether to sell a very successful business that I had founded 17 years earlier and nurtured to a position of prominence in the industry. Why I was struggling with this decision was a matter of passion. I didn't recognize it at the time, but hindsight is always 20/20. I prayed intently about the decision, and I sought counsel from trusted advisors and my family.

A pivotal point in the process was a conversation with my oldest daughter, Liisa. She was at home on break from her graduate studies and we went for a drive together. We spoke about the decision-making process, and she asked me a key question which helped me clarify my thinking: "What's the most compelling reason for you to sell the business?"

I thought for a while and then I said, "I recognize that I don't have a passion for this business."

I had come to that realization as a result of consummating a $750,000 transaction with a large power company in Connecticut. When it was completed, I just said "So what?"

Liisa told me that my words blew her away. She said, "Ever since I was a little girl, Dad, you always told me to follow my bliss, my passion. You said if I did that, I'd find happiness, fulfillment, and success. Dad, you haven't done that, and I think you should."

As my own words came back to haunt me, I knew in the very depths of my soul what the decision should be. That conversation gave me the courage to sell my business, follow my bliss, and discover my passion.

Now that I was free, I had an important question to answer: What was my bliss, my passion?

I wasn't sure, so I decided that I would take six months, a year, or whatever it took to find out what I really "wanted to do when I grew up." Through prayer and reflection, I concluded that what had brought me the most joy in life was mentoring other successful men and women, and helping them discover their abilities and their unlimited potential.

How would you answer the question, "What is my true passion?" How far are you willing to go to find it?

As I worked through my crisis of meaning, I discovered that the most fulfilling goals in life flow from who we are. In order to answer the nagging questions of meaning in your life, you need to be able to answer the most basic question: Who am I, really? Understanding who you really are is the foundation for building a fulfilling, meaningful life. When you have answered that question, you will be able to build on that understanding a purpose and mission that will lead to a life of significance.

Who are you, really? Do you need to take a three-month journey to a mountaintop in Tibet to discover the answer to that question? You might find it there, but you might just as easily find it in the silence of your own inner space. You don't need to go any farther if you know the right questions to ask and take the time to answer them carefully and honestly.

The best place I have found to start, and the place I continually return to, is what I call my source of true joy. Of all that life has to offer, what truly brings you the most joy? What makes you happiest? What makes you smile deep inside? What are your favorite aspects of being who you are? By listing these wellsprings of happiness, you will begin to identify your "bliss."

When you find it and drink deeply, you can live out your passion as an everyday expression of who you are. Make a list today of five genuine sources of joy – things that make you happy just thinking about them.

As for me, I find joy in being true to myself, and in honoring God's presence in my life and the world. I find joy in my quest to live a worthy life. I experience joy in loving my family. I rejoice in learning and growing, and in giving more than I receive. I take joy in mentoring others, and helping them discover and fulfill their potential. These are my sources of true joy!

What are yours?

1.
2.
3.
4.
5.

## Part II: Your Personal Values

There was a time in my life when I was experiencing real financial success but little or no personal satisfaction. After careful reflection, I realized that the goal of financial success alone did not reflect my real values; I needed more significance. I realized that my goals had to flow from my real values if they were to bring me the satisfaction I sought.

Libraries are stacked to the rafters with books that tell you what you want to hear – that organization, goal-setting, and continual improvement all help you get what you want. They do. The trouble, I find, is that most of those omit what ought to be the first order of business: defining what you truly want. You need to know what matters most to you in order to set new goals aimed at attaining the peace, balance, and true success you desire. Whenever you use energy to accomplish goals that have no meaning for you, you begin to lose the true motivation that comes from a sense of purpose.

It's time, then, to define your true values. How do you identify your core values, the things that matter most to you? One way is to be on the lookout for the passion in your life. What evokes your deepest emotions and elicits your unwavering commitment? These are the signposts that guide you to understand what you really value.

The following questions will expand your insights and help you understand more fully the spectrum of your own personal values.

1. What are the three greatest personal strengths you see in yourself that you would like to develop over the next three years?
    1.
    2.
    3.


2. What are the three greatest opportunities in your life you would like to capture over the next three years?
    1.
    2.
    3.


3. What are the three greatest dangers you would like to avoid or eliminate in the next three years?
    1.
    2.
    3.

4. If we were meeting together three years from now and looking back, what would have happened for you to be able to tell me that these three years had been great ones, filled with true success and real significance for you?
   1.
   2.
   3.

When you have identified what matters most to you, your true values, you have a foundation upon which to build a life of true significance.

**Part 3: Your Unique Talents**
Wouldn't it be great to be able to greet each day with enthusiasm because you know it will be filled with things you love to do? Is that even possible without being on vacation?

One key to living each day with joy and enthusiasm is recognizing and working with your own unique talents and abilities. Unfortunately, our society focuses more on identifying people's deficits rather than their strengths. We are taught, in a misguided sense of modesty, not to talk about what we do well.

After years of focusing on their weaknesses, many people have difficulty identifying or articulating their strengths. If you spend a lifetime working on your weaknesses, however, you might end up with nothing but strong weaknesses! In recognizing your unique talents and abilities, you take the first step toward optimizing them.

Your unique talents and abilities will serve you well if you identify, maximize, and leverage them. Each of us is more productive when we are doing what we do best. If our goal is to maximize our personal potential, focusing on our gifts is essential.

We feel a greater sense of significance when we are making a contribution that flows uniquely from our identity. We also enjoy doing things we do well, which means that working within our unique talents makes for a more joyful life.

How do we get our lives and careers on track so that we are in that "zone" – the joyful, productive place where we are doing productively what we enjoy and do well?

> 1) Begin by listing those things you do very well that seem practically effortless. What do you do extremely well that differentiates you from others? You do these things so

well you even feel energized by doing them. These are your unique talents.

2) Next, list the things you do well but require more effort and concentration. You're able to do these things excellently, but you do not experience the boundless energy you have for those activities which lie within your unique talents.

3) Now, list the things in your life that you do adequately but not well. You struggle with these things, and although you may be competent at doing these activities, they drain your energy reserves. These are definitely not your gifts.

4) Finally, list the things that you do poorly. These things cause you frustration and fatigue. Simply thinking about doing these things makes you tired. These energy leaks are things that you should avoid at all costs.

5) Decide now to hold every opportunity up to this unique talents yardstick. Ask yourself, "How effectively does this opportunity utilize my unique talents and gifts?" Will I enjoy this and do it well, or will I struggle unnecessarily? If an opportunity lines up with your unique

talents and personal gifts, it can help leverage and maximize your potential. If it is on the second list, something you can do excellently, this is another area worthy of your investment of time and energy. You will be effective and productive working in these areas. If it is on your third list, those things you are competent at but will take more energy and fuel less enthusiasm, consider carefully if it is the right opportunity for you. It may not be. Lastly, if it is on your fourth list, things that you struggle with and drain your energy, you'll do well to pass on it. These are the things to simplify, automate, delegate, or eliminate. Put them on a "stop doing" list.

Once you become keenly aware of your unique talents and how positively they impact your success, you will be in a better position to say "no" to the things that slow you down and hold you back, and say "yes" to the opportunities that best fit you as an individual. In this way, you can multiply your effectiveness and realize much more of your potential.

You'll know you're there working in that "zone" when you wake up in the morning filled with enthusiasm for the day ahead—and you're not on vacation! You'll experience more of the joy and fulfillment that we all want in our lives.

## Chapter One Recap

## SELF-IMAGE: Who are you, really?

1. Identify your **sources of true joy**. They will guide you to a fuller understanding of who you are.

2. Identify your most important **personal values**. What you believe in most deeply will guide you in understanding your purpose.

3. Identify your **unique talents**. Knowing what you do best will guide you toward your life's mission.

## Chapter Two

"Your vision will become clear only when you can look into your own heart."
– *Carl Jung*

# VISION:
# What is Your Purpose in Life?

## STEP #2 IS KNOWING YOUR PURPOSE

**Part One: The Power of Vision**
Vision stirs the soul and lifts the human spirit. Inspired vision will even cause people to lay down their lives. It creates a wave of passion that floods the senses, drowns fear, and carries ordinary people to extraordinary heights of human achievement.

A great example of the power of vision is the epic film, *Spartacus*, starring Kirk Douglas. It tells the story of the Roman slave, Spartacus, who labors for the Roman Empire while dreaming that one day slavery would end. Spartacus is sentenced to death after an altercation with a Roman guard, but is then spared by Batiatus, a broker of gladiators.

Spartacus trains in the arts of combat at Batiatus's gladiatorial academy. One day, two powerful men arrive from Rome, one with his wife, the other with his fiancée. The women asked to be entertained: they want to see two fights to the death. Spartacus fights a skilled gladiator who wins the fight but will not kill him; the Romans execute the gladiator for showing mercy to Spartacus.

Spartacus is enraged at the thought of being forced to fight for the entertainment of spoiled women. He leads a slave revolt that eventually spreads over half of Italy. Though outnumbered and poorly armed, Spartacus and his men go into battle against several legions of Roman soldiers and defeat them. Spartacus stands on the brink of victory when he and his army of slaves are forced into the boot of Italy and surrounded by two armies of Roman soldiers led by Commander Marcus Crassus.

Crassus knows that Spartacus is the leader of the revolt, but has never seen him. In a dramatic scene, Crassus stands before the surrounded slaves and says, "The penalty for insurrection against Rome is death on a cross." He promises that if the slaves will identify Spartacus, they will be spared. At that moment, Spartacus himself stands up and says, "I am Spartacus!" Nevertheless, another slave stands up and says, "I am Spartacus!" and then every other slave stands up and proclaims, "I am Spartacus!"

As each man stands up, he signs his own death warrant. In the final scenes, we see a long road lined with crosses with the bodies of Spartacus and his followers nailed to them.

What caused those men to give up their lives willingly? Spartacus was an inspiring leader, without question, but those men did not give up their lives for a man. They gave up their lives for their shared vision of freedom for themselves and their children. In the very last scene, Spartacus's wife stands beneath him as he hangs on the cross, and she holds up their child saying, "He will live as a free man, Spartacus."

That is the power of vision.

Vision raises us to new heights of motivation and commitment, and to new levels of effort and achievement. Vision, I believe, is the wellspring of personal fulfillment.

A vision of religious freedom is what caused 120 passengers to brave 67 days on the storm-tossed North Atlantic in a sailing vessel just 113 feet long by 26 feet wide, filled beyond capacity. The ship they were on was strong enough to withstand the rough seas, but the real strength was in the vision and faith of those within her—the pilgrims who landed in Plymouth, Massachusetts, in 1620 on the *Mayflower*.

A vision of walking on the moon inspired the technology that allowed astronaut Neil Armstrong to take "one small step for man; one giant leap for mankind."

A vision of reuniting with family or completing important unfinished work allowed Dr. Viktor Frankl and countless others to survive the atrocities of Hitler's death camps.

Vision crystallizes human values that inspire unusual levels of commitment, intrinsic motivation, faith, and purposeful action. Values are the turbo chargers of human emotion. When tapped, values allow individuals, organizations, and communities to break the chains of our self-imposed psychological limitations. Vision creates enthusiasm. *Enthusiasm* comes from the Greek word for *divine inspiration* or "the god within."

Vision is the quality that allows individuals to tap into the divine inspiration within each of us. That is what leads us not only to great heights of achievement, but to a life of significance and personal fulfillment as well.

Vision is essential to leadership. With it, individuals, organizations, communities, and countries flourish. Without it, they perish.

My vision for our business is bigger than I am. The greatest power and potential of vision is realized when it is transformed from a personal vision to a shared vision.

Our shared vision for our business reads...

> "We positively impact our world by freeing the human spirit and releasing its potential through the development of effective, empowered leaders who responsibly and enthusiastically serve the needs of others through the actualization of worthwhile, predetermined, personal and community goals, creating the endless flow of abundance intended to be enjoyed by all."

Our vision is a "wow" for us! Working together and striving to make our shared vision a reality validates our purpose and adds true meaning to our work and our lives. Our vision causes us, individually and collectively, to stretch ourselves beyond our psychological limitations to new and higher levels of performance. With each stretch, we reach greater personal actualization. With each stretch, we appreciate more fully our potential.

Each accomplishment motivates us to higher levels of achievement, success, and greater fulfillment of our vision.

Our vision creates a reverence in each of us for our work and our purpose. Our reverence for our work inspires our clients and prospects to value what we do, and they inevitably mirror that reverence back to us. When you fully appreciate the value of your work, others will, too.

This quote from George Bernard Shaw has inspired me:

> "This is the true joy in life… being used for a purpose recognized by yourself as a mighty one… being a force of Nature instead of a feverish, selfish little clod of ailments and grievances complaining that the world will not devote itself to making you happy… I am of the opinion that my life belongs to the whole community and as long as I live, it is my privilege to do for it whatever I can. I want to be thoroughly used up when I die. For the harder I work, the more I live. I rejoice in life for its own sake. Life is no brief candle to me. It's a sort of splendid torch which I've got to hold up for the moment and I want to make it burn as

brightly as possible before handing it on to future generations."

The clarity of your vision will determine the brightness of the torch that you carry forward and pass on to future generations.

Futurist Joel Barker said, "Vision without action is merely a dream. Action without vision just passes the time. Vision with action can change the world."

This is my challenge to you:

Create a vision for your life—one that is so great it inspires you to a higher level of motivation and commitment than you have ever known!

**Part Two: The Importance of Purpose and Meaning**

In *Man's Search for Meaning*, a book about survival and death in the Nazi concentration camps, Viktor Frankl observes that those who lose their purpose, their perception of meaning in life, die before their time. To maintain his own focus and dignity while in one of the camps, Frankl established three clear goals that carried him through his horrifying experience:

1. To survive
2. To use his skills as a physician to help others
3. To learn something from the experience

Frankl believed that he had a choice to make with each incident, every day. He could determine his own attitude and create meaning that would help him live and inspire others. He wrote,

> "We who lived in concentration camps can remember the men who walked through the huts comforting others, giving away their last piece of bread. They may have been few in number, but they offer sufficient proof that everything can be taken from a man but one thing: the last of the human freedoms—to choose one's attitude in any given set of circumstances, to choose one's own way."[1]

The Nazis, Frankl knew, could take his possessions, his family, his life, but they could not stifle his search for meaning unless he allowed it. This was, of course, a demonstration of exceptional character by an exceptional man, but it was also the rebellious response of a person exercising the last of his human freedoms. Viktor Frankl survived the concentration camps, and in the process, inspired not just his fellow prisoners, but also his captors with his unwavering sense of meaning and purpose.

Although few of us experience such desperate circumstances, we can still lose our sense of purpose. It can happen when we lose our circle of friends and family, when we lose our sense of joy in discovery, when we face financial hardship, or when we lose the feeling of wholeness that is part of being a vital member of a community. Even in such circumstances we still can own and control our perceptions and attitudes. This understanding frees us to embark on our own lifelong search for meaning.

We can bring greater perspective to this search for meaning when we have our whole lives in view, including the inevitable end of our time here on earth. The quality of that time, and I believe the quantity, as well, can be enhanced by extending the breadth and depth of our purpose in life. We can live more fulfilling and longer lives by expanding our understanding of what we are here for—to love, to be loved, to give and to receive.

## Part Three: How Do You Want People to Remember You?

It's time to look inside yourself and define some specifics about your ideal self: who you are, what you're made of, and whom you ultimately want to be. One question that can help you discover whom you ultimately want to be is this: when your life here is over, how do you want people to remember you? What words do you hope people will hear at your funeral? What would you choose to have engraved on your headstone?

Susan B. Anthony's gravestone features the words "Liberty, Humanity, Justice, Equality." She believed in these ideals. They were the standards she strove for throughout her life. Traveling the United States and Europe, she campaigned against slavery, worked for the temperance movement, and spoke out for the rights of women. She lived for these values and died in the hope that they would be her legacy.

As far as I know, people do not list their net worth at death on their gravestones, nor do they list the awards they acquired on their journey. Instead, they choose words and symbols of faith, and make note of service in the military or civic groups important to them. They list family relationships—a loving father, mother, husband, wife, son, or daughter. At the end of our lives, we define ourselves by the values we believe in most and the people we love. These things represent the significance of our lives.

By asking the sobering question of what your life will ultimately mean to you and to others, you take an important step on the path to true significance. There is a big difference between success and significance. You can lead a successful life by the world's standards and not achieve a life of significance. On the other hand, you cannot achieve a life of significance without being successful, as I understand success.

Take the time to define now what would make you feel like your life was significant. Define meaning in your life now in terms of how you want people to remember you when you are gone. You will find greater direction and contentment as the real priorities in your life become clear. What do you need to do to close the gap between the way you see yourself now and how you want people to remember you? You can begin to become the person you have envisioned. Act now while you have the opportunity to live intentionally and become your best, truest, and most significant self.

## Chapter Two Recap

# VISION: What is your purpose in life?

1. A compelling **vision** that guides and inspires you to fulfill your highest purpose.

2. Having a clearly defined **purpose** can bring meaning that motivates us to overcome even the most desperate circumstances.

3. Our life's purpose flows from **who we truly are**.

4. The question **"How do I want people to remember me?"** can help you define who you are and hope to become.

SEVEN STEPS TO A LIFE OF SIGNIFICANCE

## Chapter Three

"The two most important days in your life are the day you are born and the day you find out why."
– *Mark Twain*

# MISSION:
# How will you fulfill your purpose?

## STEP 3 IS KNOWING YOUR MISSION

**Part One: The Importance of Writing your Personal Mission Statement**

If you have read this far, I sincerely hope you have done the hard work of identifying your sources of joy, personal values, and unique talents. I hope you have taken the time to create a compelling and meaningful vision for your life and to understand your purpose. If you have not, I urge you to stop reading right now and go back to do that foundational work.

Have you heard about the man who struggled and climbed for years to reach the top of the ladder, only to find that the ladder was leaning against the wrong wall? I don't want you to be that person. Be sure you have your values, vision, and purpose clearly defined before you go on to write your personal life mission.

If you have truly tapped into your sources of joy, if your vision for your life inspires you deeply, and if your purpose fills you with enthusiasm, it is imperative that you have a *mission*. A mission is the means by which you will fulfill your purpose. Your values tell you *why*. Your vision and purpose tell you *what*. Your mission tells you *how*. A vision is only a dream until we determine how we will fulfill it.

John F. Kennedy cast a vision for the nation of putting a man on the moon, and NASA developed the Apollo mission. Martin Luther King, Jr., set forth a vision for freedom and equality for all people, and then made it his mission to advance that vision through the Civil Rights Movement. In 1962, J.C.R. Licklider envisioned a worldwide network of computers he called the "Galactic Network." Many others made it their mission over the twenty years that followed to create what has become the World Wide Web.

Your mission will make your vision a reality. In the process, you will experience the joy along the way of seeing what you have envisioned become reality, step by step. Life is not a destination but a journey. Having a mission gives meaning, drive, and satisfaction along the way. You don't have to wait until the end to know that you are succeeding in living a life of significance as you have defined it! When you are in the process of accomplishing your life's mission, you can enjoy significance and success along the way.

Once you have a mission for your life, making decisions will be simpler. Your mission will become the yardstick for measuring every opportunity. By this measure you will determine the people you bring into your life, the activities you do, and the places you go. Your mission will determine your goals and plans. It will become a lens that filters out the things that don't really matter, helping you stay focused on what ultimately does matter. Your mission will become a compass to guide you toward the fulfillment of your vision, helping you keep steadily on the path.

## Part Two: How My Mission Statement Led to a New and Fulfilling Career

Some twenty years ago, equipped with a personal mission statement and a purpose, I began to travel the country seeking an opportunity that would allow me to fulfill that mission and purpose. I was struck by the abundance of opportunity. It was everywhere! The challenge was finding one that was congruent with my values.

Eventually I responded to an ad in the *Wall Street Journal* for a company called Leadership Management International. I made arrangements to visit Waco, Texas, and meet a man named Tony Stigliano. I knew that something was right about the company the moment I walked through the door. I felt very much at home with the friendly people and their warm, positive attitudes. As I learned more about the company, I recognized that the values at LMI were very congruent with mine. In our concluding meeting, Tony Stigliano asked me, "Is LMI what you're looking for?"

I pulled out a 3x5 card that I carried with me. On it, I had written my personal mission statement. I read it to him:

> "To enjoy a happy, fulfilling and purposeful life by remaining committed to a personal and professional goals program that will allow me to develop my physical, mental, and spiritual gifts to their fullest potential. To use my talents in engaged and focused activities that will enhance the quality of life, promote self-esteem, develop self-confidence, personal growth, and the fulfillment of human potential in myself, my family, my associates and those that I have the privilege to serve."

Tony smiled and said, "I think you've found what you're looking for."

He told me that I'd do well in this business because I was already a product of the product. I immediately thought Tony was a man of discerning taste and good judgment! I honestly thought that I was a product of the product, too; however, I quickly came to learn that I was not. That is an ongoing process. It is never-ending. It is a journey, not a destination.

I began my journey with LMI in August of 1993. It has been an exciting voyage of discovery for me, as well as for my associates and our clients. The vision that I articulated in my mission and purpose has become reality. I am happier, more fulfilled, and more purposeful in my personal and professional life than I have ever been.

This is a challenging business. I built more character in the first two years than I did in the previous ten. I had to overcome many obstacles, but the biggest—the very biggest—was me. It gets lonely when you start out in a new business. I've successfully started businesses before, but I had forgotten how difficult it was.

I told my wife it must be like having a baby; once it's done, you forget the pain. She assured me very quickly that it was NOTHING like having a baby! Nonetheless, it was difficult.

I'm a very confident person, yet there have been many times when I had to fight serious self-doubt. I had to keep moving forward one small step at a time toward the accomplishment of my goals.

As I became more of a product of the product, I gained confidence in myself and in what we do. With increased confidence, I became more successful at sharing the gift that we have to offer our clients.

The more that I share the gift, the more appreciative I become of the power we have to transform people's lives.

In this world of great opportunity, have you found the ones that are congruent with your values and will allow you to fulfill your purpose?

From the work you have done so far, you know who you are and have identified your purpose in life. Now it is time to write your personal mission statement.

## Part Three: Writing your Personal Mission Statement

By now you have a vision of what you want your life to be. How will you fulfill that vision? Answer that, and you have your *mission*.

Your mission statement should cover all areas of your life:

- Home and Family
- Spiritual and Ethical
- Physical and Health
- Financial and Career
- Mental and Educational
- Social and Cultural

In the remainder of your time on earth, what will you accomplish in each of these areas to fulfill your vision and your purpose?

Write down each of the six areas listed above on a piece of paper. Where do you see yourself twenty years from now in each area? What do you hope your family life will be like when you are fifty-five? Where do you want to be financially when you retire? What kind of health do you envision for yourself at seventy?

Questions like these that focus on the long-term help you identify what you need to accomplish to create the life you have envisioned.

Your mission should be uniquely yours. There is no template because each of us has a unique vision and purpose for our lives. To give you an idea of what a life mission statement might look like, however, I'll share what mine looks like today:

> "To live a meaningful and significant life by developing and using my God-given talents to create a flow of spiritual and financial abundance to do as much good as I can for my family, friends, clients, church, and community for as long as I live."

Your mission statement should be specific enough to fulfill your personal vision, but broad enough to drive a wealth of goals in each area of life. It should reflect your personal values and vision so compellingly that when you read it, you see the person you really want to be.

**Your Personal Mission Statement:**

_____
_____
_____
_____
_____

_____

_____

_____

_____

**Part Four: How to Use Your Mission Statement to Fuel Motivation and Fulfill Your Vision**
You may have heard of company retreats where executives gather to formulate vision and mission statements. They often come away with inspiring statements about what they envision for their company and how they hope to fulfill that vision. Sometimes the statements are printed, framed, and hung on the wall in the executive conference room. More often, they are filed in a drawer and forgotten. In most cases, the problem is that the people who wrote those statements do not have a process to drive them.

How can you make sure that the hard work you have put into your vision and mission statements leads you to the life of significance you seek?

> *First*, don't file it in a drawer. When you are confident in what you have written, print it out and post it where you will see it daily, as a constant reminder.

***Second***, read your vision and mission statement aloud to yourself every day. Twice a day is better! Memorize it and internalize it. Firmly fix it in your consciousness so that it becomes the guiding principle of your everyday life. See it as the inevitable outcome of being who you are.

***Third***, begin the search for opportunities that match your mission, that utilize your unique talents, and that live up to your values. Once you have identified the best opportunities, hold each one up to your mission statement to see how well it fits. Let your mission statement be the measuring stick for every opportunity. Let it be your guide for whom you bring into your life, what you choose to do, and where you choose to go. Let it be the gatekeeper of your personal and professional life.

***Fourth***, maintain a steady focus on your progress toward realizing your vision and your personal mission. Remember that success is a journey, not a destination. By focusing on progress, you ensure that your journey is leading you in the direction you have chosen.

Unlike most people, you have a clear vision of the life to which you aspire, and a mission that leads toward its fulfillment. You have a strong sense of purpose. All the self-discovery work you have done will be a huge asset now. It will ensure that everything you choose contributes toward building the life of significance you have envisioned.

## Chapter Three Recap

# MISSION: How will you fulfill your purpose?

1. Writing your **personal mission statement** answers the question "how will I fulfill my vision?" and keeps you focused on what matters most.

2. A personal mission statement can lead you to a career and future that is not only successful but truly significant.

3. Your mission statement should be **specific** enough to fulfill your personal vision, but **broad** enough to drive goals in all areas of life.

4. Read your mission statement daily and actively use it to search for and qualify opportunities.

## Chapter Four

"Whether you think you can, or you think you can't, you're right"
— *Henry Ford*

# LIFE STRATEGIES: How Will You Accomplish Your Mission?

### Part One: Attitude Is Everything

I believe that my personal attitude is a crucial factor in the success I have enjoyed in my life, and that it will be a key element in your future success as well.

Attitude is key and the good news is that each of us has the ability to choose our own attitude, even in the most adverse situation. Consider carefully the true story of a man named Jerry[9]

> Jerry is the kind of guy you love to hate. He is always in a good mood and always has something positive to say. When someone would ask him how he was doing, he would reply, "If I were any better, I would be twins!"

He was a unique manager because he had several waiters who had followed him around from restaurant to restaurant. The reason the waiters followed Jerry was because of his attitude. He was a natural motivator. If an employee was having a bad day, Jerry was there telling the employee how to look on the positive side of the situation.

Seeing this style really made me curious, so one day I went up to Jerry and said to him, "I don't get it! You can't be a positive person all of the time. How do you do it?"

Jerry replied, "Each morning I wake up and say to myself, Jerry, you have two choices today. You can choose to be in a good mood or you can choose to be in a bad mood. I choose to be in a good mood. Each time something bad happens, I can choose to be a victim or I can choose to learn from it. I choose to learn from it. Every time someone comes to me complaining, I can choose to accept their complaining or I can point out the positive side of life. I choose the positive side of life."

"Yeah, right; it's not that easy," I protested.

"Yes, it is," Jerry said. "Life is all about choices. When you cut away all the junk, every situation is a choice. You choose how to react to situations. You choose how people will affect your mood. You choose to be in a good mood or bad mood. The bottom line: It's your choice how you live life."

I reflected on what Jerry said. Soon thereafter, I left the restaurant industry to start my own business. We lost touch, but I often thought about him when I made a choice about life instead of reacting to it.

Several years later, I heard that Jerry did something you are never supposed to do in the restaurant business: he left the back door open one morning and was held up at gunpoint by three armed robbers. While trying to open the safe, his hand, shaking from nervousness, slipped off the combination. The robbers panicked and shot him.

Luckily, Jerry was found relatively quickly and rushed to the local trauma center. After 18 hours of surgery and weeks of intensive care, Jerry was released from the hospital with fragments of the bullets still in his body.

I saw Jerry about six months after the accident. When I asked him how he was, he replied, "If I were any better, I'd be twins. Wanna see my scars?"

I declined to see his wounds, but did ask him what had gone through his mind as the robbery took place. "The first thing that went through my mind was that I should have locked the back door," Jerry replied. "Then, as I lay on the floor, I remembered that I had two choices: I could choose to live or I could choose to die. I chose to live."

"Weren't you scared? Did you lose consciousness?" I asked.

Jerry continued, "The paramedics were great. They kept telling me I was going to be fine. But when they wheeled me in the ER and I saw the expressions on the faces of the doctors and nurses, I got really scared. In their eyes, I read 'he's a dead man.' I knew I needed to take action."

"What did you do?" I asked.

"Well, there was a big, burly nurse shouting questions at me," said Jerry. She asked if I was allergic to anything.

"'Yes,' I replied.

"The doctors and nurses stopped working as they waited for my reply. I took a deep breath and yelled, 'Bullets!' Over their laughter, I told them, 'I am choosing to live. Operate on me as if I am alive, not dead.'"

Jerry lived thanks to the skill of his doctors, but also because of his amazing attitude. I learned from him that every day we have the choice to live fully.

Attitude, after all, is everything.

Now we'll look at some strategies for developing and maintaining the positive mental attitude necessary to achieve our full potential for the happiness, fulfillment, and true success we all desire.

## Part Two: Strategies for Developing and Maintaining a Positive Mental Attitude

Paul J. Meyer, a pioneer in the field of personal development, said, "Goal-setting is the strongest human force for self-motivation." Setting clear and compelling goals is our greatest tool for developing and maintaining a positive mental attitude. Goal setting creates a sense of purpose and gives you a plan and path for moving forward.

I currently track ten hours per month working on goal development in my personal plan of action. Watch what happens to your attitude when you clearly define your goals, values, and purpose in life! We'll work on the specifics of goal-setting in chapter five.

The second strategy for developing and maintaining a positive mental attitude is to focus on your progress. Focusing on your progress and the incremental achievement of action steps instills confidence, increases energy, and reinforces a positive attitude.

Many individuals are conditioned to focus on the ideal or on perfection instead of the progressive realization of their goals. These individuals rob themselves of the joy, fulfillment, happiness, achievement, and satisfaction that the goal setting process is intended to bring. Their focus on the ideal or on perfection causes them to experience stress, frustration, low self-image, lack of confidence, and unhappiness regardless of their level of achievement.

There is a permanent gap between perfection and your actual achievement because, like the horizon, perfection keeps moving. It is a mental construct. It seems real in your mind but it never becomes reality. If you persist in perfectionist thinking, comparing your achievements to perfection, you will always be disappointed and experience negative emotion no matter what you achieve.

Those who experience the true joy of the goal-setting process are "progressive thinkers" who compare their achievement to where they began the journey. By measuring backward instead of forward, "progressive thinkers" maximize their confidence and energy. At Leadership Dynamics, Inc., we cultivate a positive attitude by focusing on our progress daily, weekly, monthly, quarterly, and yearly.

Each day, I take note of my accomplishments to validate my progress toward my goals. This habit allows me to protect my confidence, energy, and positive mental attitude. All of my team members also focus on their progress daily and weekly. For us, focusing on progress rather than perfection is part of our culture and the catalyst for our positive attitudes.

Are you setting an example for your associates, family, and friends by practicing "progressive thinking" and continuously focusing on progress? If you are, congratulations! If you are not, what action will you take today to develop the habit of focusing on your progress?

The third strategy for maintaining a positive mental attitude is to develop an experimental mindset. In other words, don't think about life in terms of successes and failures. Think about your life in terms of things that work for you and things that don't.

The experimental mindset is a common characteristic of most unusually successful individuals throughout history. Thomas Edison was a perfect example of an individual with an experimental mindset. When asked how he could keep working on the development of the incandescent light bulb after failing so many times, he responded, "If I find 10,000 ways something won't work, I haven't failed. I am not discouraged, because every wrong attempt discarded is another step forward."

An experimental mindset allows you to practice the habit of maintaining emotional equanimity. It helps you avoid the wide swings in your emotions that individuals who think only in terms of success or failure often experience.

One of my clients puts it this way: "The highs are so high, and the lows are so low!" Maintaining emotional equanimity allows you to be more mentally disciplined and capable of practicing the behaviors that have consistently produced true and lasting success throughout history. Start thinking experimentally. I guarantee it will improve your attitude!

## Part Three: The Balancing Act – Your Wheel of True Success

Have you ever been driving your car on the highway, and as you accelerate to cruising speed you begin to feel the car shudder or the steering wheel wobble? Chances are that is not the inspiring, smooth ride you were hoping for. In fact, it can be so unsettling you move over into the slow lane.

One common reason for vibrations of that kind is tire imbalance. If you take your car to a garage, the technician can put your tires on a balancing machine. The machine rotates the tire at high speeds and carefully measures any imbalance. The technician then adds small weights strategically to achieve optimal balance. The result? A smoother ride at higher speeds.

Like the wheels of an automobile, your life has to be balanced in order to move forward smoothly. A balanced life allows you to achieve and enjoy more in life, and to share those benefits with others. Achieving life balance, however, doesn't come automatically.

We begin by assessing our current balance, and then go on to make adjustments to achieve optimal performance. There are six areas of life to consider: physical and health; mental and educational; family and home; spiritual and ethical; social and cultural; and financial and career.

Each area supports the others, and with a good measure of each, we can look forward to a smoother ride and more rapid progress.

If you picture your life as a wheel, you are the hub, the center of the action. Radiating from this hub are the six vital spokes. The challenge is to define your level of success in each sector of the wheel. Rate yourself, on a scale of one to ten, in each of the following areas:

1. Physical and Health
2. Mental and Educational
3. Family and Home
4. Spiritual and Ethical

5. Social and Cultural
6. Financial and Career

Each of these sectors is critical to defining who you are. They help identify your areas of personal strength and needs for personal development. What areas of life could you improve in order to achieve greater balance?

Most people's wheels require continual adjustments and constant improvement. Balance will look different at each stage of life. In college, a balanced life requires more attention to the educational area (and self-restraint in the social!). After college, most people will spend a greater proportion of time kick-starting their career. After marriage, family and home will necessarily take up a greater percentage of your time.

In each stage of life, however, you will benefit by giving appropriate time to each area. A young employee aspiring to become a manager may need to work overtime, but she still needs to exercise and eat right. A couple with young children may find that their lives revolve around the nursery, but they still need to get out and spend time with people their own age. A successful entrepreneur about to go public with his first company still has a need to balance career success with attention to his family and community life.

It's not about perfection. It's about developing a well-rounded life that helps you achieve more of what matters to you. Re-assess your life balance again and again as you move forward in your quest for a life of significance.

**Part Four: Eliminating Energy Leaks**
If you have looked carefully at each area of your life and determined which of them needs more attention, you probably realize that creating balance will require a commitment of *time* and *energy*. For each of us, time and energy are finite commodities, and we all have to manage them carefully. You will find plenty of material written about managing your time (and that is vital), but less about managing your energy.

Paul J. Meyer said that a bucket with a small hole in it gets just as empty as a bucket that is intentionally kicked over. This is true of both time and energy. If you had a serious leak in your gas tank, I'm sure you'd want to fix it before putting more fuel into it. In order to safeguard your energy for the activities most important to you, you need to identify what I call "energy leaks." Energy leaks are things that drain your physical and emotional strength and rob you of the stamina required to pursue truly meaningful goals.

They are the undone projects or neglected tasks that eat away at your motivation every time you think of them. They're things like untidy lawns and over-stuffed garages that hold everything except your cars. They are the employees that you know just aren't fitting in, and yet you put off taking action. They are the out-of-control schedule, the disorganized and frustrated people around you, and the coworkers who expect you to boost their energy. They are also the goals you pursue that have no meaning for you. These are all energy leaks. They deplete your strength and may leave you without the motivation to do the things that matter most.

The good news is that you can take action *now* to stop the energy leaks. Take some time alone to think about what projects, activities, issues, or relationships in your life are sapping your strength. What energy leaks do you need to eliminate so that you can focus on achieving the things that matter most to you? Identify five specific issues you can address now: things left undone or annoyances not dealt with that undermine your motivation and drain your physical and emotional strength.

List specific action steps you can take to address each, and set target dates for achieving them. Take action on at least one of them today. Build your confidence and restore motivation by identifying and eliminating energy leaks, starting now!

|  | Action Step | Target Date |
|---|---|---|
| 1. | _____ |  |
| 2. | _____ |  |
| 3. | _____ |  |
| 4. | _____ |  |
| 5. | _____ |  |

**Part Five: The Life Enhancement and Extension Exercise**

A life of significance is more about how we live than how long we live. No one wants to die before it's time, and we'd all like to enjoy the greatest possible quality of life for as long as we can. Besides health issues and accidents, the three most significant reasons people die before their time are:

1. A lack of friends
2. A lack of money
3. A lack of purpose

Loneliness, poverty, and a lack of purpose are three things we'd like very much to avoid as we age, if we want both quality of life and longevity. The Life Enhancement and Extension Exercise below will help you find the keys not only to maximizing your lifespan, but building significance into your life now, rather than later.

1. Write down your current age.

2. Add five years to your current age and write down that number.

3. To what age do you expect to live? Write down this number. If you are like most people, you probably have a number in your head that has been there for a long time based on family history or other factors. People are usually unaware of how much we organize our lives to accommodate that number!

4. In the six areas listed below, consider the specifications you envision for your life the year before you expect to die. In what physical and mental condition do you hope to be (e.g., "I will be reading two hours a day," or, "I will be walking three miles a day")? Be specific (blood pressure, pulse, weight, etc.). What kind of family relationships do you envision? Describe the kind of spiritual life you will have, and your circle of friends. Consider what level of financial comfort you will have obtained.

Establish desired specifications for each area of your life. Write down your answers.

- Physical and Health
- Mental and Educational
- Family and Home
- Spiritual and Ethical
- Social and Cultural
- Financial and Career

5. After filling in these specifications, think about what would happen if you were really experiencing those conditions the year before you died. If you were, for instance, walking three miles a day, enjoying an active circle of friends, surrounded by family and connected with a worshipping community, what impact would that have? How many years could these activities and relationships add to your life span?

To help you answer that, consider the following:

Even small changes in your lifestyle can net significant increases in longevity. Boosting your intake of fruits and vegetables to five portions a day, for instance, could add three years; not smoking, five years; increasing exercise even moderately could add another three.[2]

People over 50 who approached aging positively and proactively were found to live an average of 7.5 years longer than those who took a pessimistic view.[3]

Friendships have been shown to have a significant impact on longevity, even greater than that of family.[4]

Those with more education and a higher socio-economic status have been shown to have a better chance of living longer, healthier lives.[5]

Among older Americans, those who attended religious services once a week or more had significantly higher survival rates.[6]

*The British Medical Journal* published a study in which workers who retired at 65 lived an average of eight years longer than those who retired at 55.[7]

A University of Michigan study explored the role of purpose and meaning in longevity, and concluded, "Older people may live longer if they are able to maintain a sense of control over the role that is most important to them."[10] A related study concluded that seniors who worked in their community as volunteers even an hour a week or less than an hour a week lived longer.[8]

So, based on the conditions you identify, estimate how many years your desired life specifications would add to your lifespan. Write down your new projected lifespan.

6. What would you do with this extra time? What you would plan for your "extra" years shows whom you truly are and wish to be. Write down how you would spend your extra years. Would you travel, go back to school, play golf, volunteer, learn a language, or pursue some other life-long dream? Why wait until the last years of your life to start doing the things you dream of doing?

7. Now that you have identified what you want your life to be in your last years, what do you have to do now to end up there? Set goals in each area of life that will propel you toward the life you have envisioned.

8. Determine five-year priorities for establishing the habits that will allow you to attain your desired life specifications. Write down your five-year priorities and begin planning action steps to achieve them. Take action on your first steps, and you have made a great beginning on your journey to a life of significance!

## Chapter Four Recap

# LIFE STRATEGIES: How will you accomplish your mission?

1. Cultivating a **positive mental attitude** is crucial to our success, and we have the ability to choose our attitude in any given circumstance.

2. Setting clear and compelling **goals**, focusing on **progress**, and an **experimental mindset** are three invaluable tools for developing and maintaining a positive mental attitude.

3. Pay careful attention to **balance** in your life, knowing that a balanced life allows you to achieve more and enjoy more of what truly matters.

4. Build confidence and maintain energy by identifying and eliminating **energy leaks** in your life.

5. Identify where you hope to be at the end of your life and make the changes required now to enjoy greater longevity and quality of life.

## Chapter Five

> "Life can be pulled by goals as much as it can be pushed by drives."
> – *Viktor Frankl*

# SETTING GOALS:
# How Will You Get From Here to There?

**Part One: The Importance of Written Goals**
Henry David Thoreau said, "If you have built castles in the air, your work need not be lost; that is where they should be. Now put the foundations under them." The work you have done on your self-image, vision, and mission lays the groundwork for a life of true significance. In step 4, it is time to develop the goals that determine how you will achieve your mission and fulfill your vision—the "why" of your life.

As you ask the question "how," your long and short-range goals will start to come into view. As you advance to this next level, your goals will become clearer based on the work you have already done. As they do, it is important to consider the power of written goals.

In a recent study by Dr. Gail Matthews at Dominican University, working-age participants from various countries and professions were asked to either think about goals or to write them down. Four weeks later, the 149 participants who completed the study were asked "to rate their progress and the degree to which they had accomplished their goals." The study provided "empirical evidence that writing one's goal enhances goal achievement." Those who wrote down their goals had about 30% higher success rates. Consider each area of your life. What would a 30% increase in the achievement of your goals mean to you?

I have worked with hundreds of clients from many backgrounds and walks of life, and helped people from dozens of companies learn how to achieve their goals. With all of them—whether CEOs, managers, those who work in accounting, sales, engineering, or manufacturing—I start at the same place: clear, written goals.

Time and again I have seen their productivity at work and accomplishments at home increase dramatically as they learn about the power of writing down their goals, daily, monthly, quarterly, and beyond.

There are three reasons I find that we accomplish written goals more often than those we don't write down. The first is that the process of writing down your goals forces you to crystallize your thinking so you identify clearly what you want. You may think, "I want to spend more time with my children."

Our process for creating written goals will help you get more specific, for example, spending three evenings a week doing fun activities with the family for two hours. If you truly intend to achieve your goals, it is important that they be crystal clear.

The second reason written goals trump the unwritten is accountability. When we write down our goals we commit them to paper, raising our own level of commitment, and making it easier to share those goals with others. The Gail Matthews study referenced above found that people who wrote down their goals, formulated action commitments, shared them with a friend, and submitted regular progress reports achieved 20% more than those who only wrote them down, and 64% more than those who only thought about them.

What would 64% higher goal-achievement look like in your life?

That leads to the third advantage of written goals: tracking. Written goals are easy to track, and that is the key to goal management. When you measure progress on a regular basis, you feel motivated to keep going and you always know whether or not you are on track.

Then you can make the adjustments needed to ensure timely completion of the goal. A tracking device can be a graph, a chart, or a simple thermometer with written action steps and target dates. However you choose to do it, tracking your goals will increase your success in achieving the goals you set.

Because you are building your goals on what is most important to you—the very core of who you are and what you want to accomplish in life—isn't the work of writing them down small compared to the high return on that investment of time? As with all things, the choice is yours to make.

**Part Two: Setting S.M.A.R.T. Goals**
We've all heard about working smarter rather than harder. The best way to start is by setting smart goals. "S.M.A.R.T." is a great acronym that describes a way of setting goals that will maximize the likelihood that you will achieve them.

S.M.A.R.T. goals are:

**Specific.** The human mind is like a guided missile. Give it a specific target, and it will seek out that objective. Have you ever bought a car and then noticed that particular make and model seems to be everywhere? When you supply your mind with a clear picture, it looks for that and finds it. You can use this mental power to help you achieve your goals when you make them specific. Don't set a goal to "start running"; set a goal to train for the 5K charity run in the fall. Don't just decide that you will spend "more time with your family"; set aside three nights a week to do favorite activities with the kids. Don't resolve to just "prepare for retirement"; set specific savings and investment goals. Maximize the potential of your mind to focus on a specific target.

Vague goals produce few or no results. When you set your goals, don't think in general terms about "more," but state specifically how much more. Specify who will be involved, what you plan to do, when you will do it, how you will accomplish it, and why you are doing it. When your goal is that clear, you have a track to run on and are much more likely to reach the finish line.

**Measurable.** Specific goals lead to the achievement of measurable results. Set your goals in a way that you can track your progress. Lay out action steps that you can check off one by one. If you hope to get through that 5K charity run in the fall without a defibrillator, how will you measure your progress? If the race is in six months, how far should you be able to run in three months? (2.5 K, right?) In order to do that, how far should you be able to run in six weeks? (1.75 K).

In that case, what is the goal for three weeks from now? (Okay 1K is close enough!) So, how far should you be able to run by the end of this week? (0.3 K) Do you think you could do that? If you can, and you keep it up, you can train for that 5K enjoying success every step of the way. With specific metrics, you can make sure that every day you are on track to win.

I find that many people shy away from measurement. Why? They are afraid of accountability. They don't want to commit to specific metrics because no one wants to look bad if he fails. How will you know if you have achieved your objective if you have no way of measuring it? How will you be able to make course corrections if you don't know where you stand? Wouldn't you rather know where you are, so you can chart the best course forward?

**Attainable and Realistic.** What is the difference between attainable and realistic? Attainable goals are humanly possible. It is, for instance, humanly possible to go to the moon. Realistic goals are based on past performance, available resources, and current conditions. So going to the moon, for most of us, wouldn't qualify as a realistic goal. SMART goals are both humanly possible and realistic, considering what we've accomplished before, how much time, money, and other resources are available, and the conditions under which we are working.

That doesn't mean we don't reach high; goals should always stretch us. We look at where we've been and reach a bit further (say, a 15%-20% increase in revenues in the next quarter). "Nothing succeeds like success," said Alexandre Dumas, so set yourself up for success by setting stretch goals that are both attainable and realistic.

**Tangible.** Tangible goals are concrete. You can touch them. Many of our goals start as intangibles, For example, "I want a better relationship with my spouse," or "we want a more positive work environment." In order to make those things more concrete, ask yourself, "What would that look like?" If I had a stronger relationship with my spouse, would we go on vacations together, spend time together in the evenings, or go ballroom dancing? How often would we do those things, where, and with whom?

The relationship is intangible, but the results are tangible, and you know when you've achieved them. If we had a more positive work environment, what would that look like? Would meetings have more laughter and fewer arguments? Would people cooperate more on projects rather than avoiding one another? Would people come to work on time more often, and be absent from work less often? A positive atmosphere is hard to measure, but the results are tangible. When you set your goals, focus on tangible results.

Now is the time to set S.M.A.R.T. goals based on your personal values, vision, and mission, for each area of your life:

- Physical
- Mental
- Family
- Spiritual
- Social
- Financial

**Part Three: One Bite at a Time – Breaking Down Long-Range Goals**
Henry David Thoreau said:

> "If one advances confidently in the direction of his dreams, and endeavors to live the life which he has imagined, he will meet with a success unexpected in common hours."

When you plan a long journey on a map, there are two points you locate first: where you are now, and where you ultimately want to be. Then, studying the available roads, you choose a route that will take you to your destination. If you set out haphazardly in a general direction, you might never end up where you want to be. One thing is certain, however: you will reach the end. Setting long-term goals is really all about ending where you hope to be.

Once you have developed a clear vision of who you are and your purpose in life, once you have discovered the mission that will fulfill that vision, you can begin setting specific, measurable, attainable, realistic, and tangible (as well as intangible) goals to get there. Develop your goals by working in reverse. Start with the person you want to be when you reach the end of your journey. Take the time to think carefully about where you would like to end up in each area of life.

Financial planners do this with very careful calculations. They ask what kind of income you would like to have when you retire, and then they calculate just how much money you will need to invest each year to get there. When you know that, you can determine how much to put aside each month. You can apply the same process to each area of your life.

Are you hoping that in your last years you will have a wide circle of friends? How many people do you count as your friends now? Developing relationships requires a commitment of time. What will you need to do over the next five years to help ensure that later in life you have a vibrant and supportive social circle? Let's say you are twenty years from retirement, and want to be fit and agile in your later years, walking, running, perhaps even playing tennis. How fit are you now? How fit would you have to be in ten years in order to reach and maintain the level of fitness you hope to have when you retire?

Most of us would like to be mentally sharp in our later years. We know that a commitment to lifelong learning, especially learning new things, keeps our minds in optimal condition. How committed are you to learning new things now? What would you be able to do over the next five years to help ensure that in your later years your mind is as sharp as it can be?

Once you have a clear idea of where you want to end up, and five-year goals leading steadily in that direction, you are ready to set mid-range and short-term goals. Still working in reverse, ask yourself: if your vision is to become reality in five years, where do you need to be in four years? What do you need to be doing in two years? What do you need to accomplish in the next six months? The next three months? What do you need to do this week, and what purposeful steps forward will you take today toward realizing your vision?

Your vision is translated step by step into reality through your daily work and personal activities, the things you do. There is an old adage, "By the yard, it's hard; by the inch, it's a cinch!" Think about the longest driveway you ever shoveled or the deepest hole you ever dug. Had you listened to your fears that you might collapse before you ever dug your way to where you were going, you never would have started the job. You'd have just crawled back into bed.

Instead, you set a short-term goal, like 50 shovels-full, or maybe three feet of progress. "A goal begun is half done," and to your amazement, that progress inspired you to go further and further. Your short-term success gave you the momentum and confidence you required to work your way slowly but surely down the driveway. Every time you looked back to review your progress, rather than lament the enormity of the task ahead, you were encouraged.

The closer you got to the end, even as you grew more tired, you grew more determined and confident. That's what happens when we break down our long term goals into manageable, bite-sized increments. How do you eat an elephant? One bite at a time. When you understand this, you realize that fulfilling your life's mission is very much about what you do today. Being able to connect the dots between what you are doing today and your vision for the future is the key to maintaining your enthusiasm, motivation, and continuous progress to the achievement of your goals.

Andrew Carnegie, a great American entrepreneur and extraordinary philanthropist, said: "The older I get, the less attention I pay to what people say. I simply watch what they do." Make your actions today the most profound statements about the person you ultimately want to be.

**Part Four: Enjoying Success Along the Way**
American tennis player and social activist Arthur Ashe said, "Success is a journey not a destination." He knew well what it meant to experience success not as a goal at the end of your life, but as the result of choices you make along the way.

Arthur Ashe was born in Richmond, Virginia, in 1943, and when he was just seven years old, his mother died. Arthur's father raised him and his younger brother while working as a handyman and policeman.

Like many boys, Arthur wanted to play football, but his father wouldn't allow it because of his slight build. As it happened, though, the family's home was located at the Brookfield Playground, and they had a tennis court. Ashe began to play tennis there, and eventually excelled at it in school. *Sports Illustrated* recognized him as a promising young player, and he got a tennis scholarship to UCLA. He became the first African-American player to be chosen for a U.S. Davis Cup team. In 1965, he won the NCAA singles title and helped UCLA win the NCAA team championship.

Arthur Ashe went on to a distinguished tennis career that earned him many honors as well as praise from tennis legend Jack Kramer who listed him as one of the best 21 tennis players of all time.[i] He is the only African American man to have won the singles title at the U.S. Open, the Australian Open, and Wimbledon. For some, this might have been success enough, the end of a journey and the fulfillment of a dream.

Not for Arthur Ashe. In 1972, he was preparing to play in the South African Open when the South African government denied him a visa. Ashe saw this not merely as a setback, but as an opportunity to act on his core values. He used the incident to draw attention to South Africa's policy of apartheid, responding to the circumstance by working for the cause of social justice. He took part in a delegation of African Americans who went to South Africa as the country began the process of integration. He later protested apartheid outside the South African Embassy in Washington and was arrested.

In 1979, to everyone's surprise, Arthur had a heart attack. He had a quadruple bypass, and a few months later, was just about to resume his tennis career. On a family trip to Egypt, he again experienced chest pains that sent him back to the hospital for more surgery to correct the previous bypass. Heart disease brought Ashe's career as a tennis player to a close, but it did not diminish his success as a person.

Once again, he used the opportunity for good. He became part of a public awareness campaign to help others understand the hereditary nature of heart disease; if an athlete in top condition could have a heart attack, then everyone needed to take heart health seriously.

Retired from tennis, Ashe commented for ABC Sports, wrote for *Time* magazine, and founded the National Junior Tennis League. He became captain of the U.S. Davis Cup team, and in 1985, became a member of the International Tennis Hall of Fame.

In 1986, Ashe and his wife adopted a baby girl. Just two years later, Arthur lost feeling and movement in his right arm. After extensive testing, doctors found that he had toxoplasmosis, a disease often found in people with HIV. Ashe's doctors concluded that he had contracted the virus from blood transfusions during earlier heart surgery.

Knowing that news of his illness would soon become public, Ashe himself came forward and announced that he had HIV. Then, once again using adversity for good, he went to work raising public awareness about HIV and its prevention. Later he created the Arthur Ashe Foundation for the Defeat of AIDS and the Arthur Ashe Institute for Urban Health.

In February of 1993, at the age of fifty, Arthur Ashe died of AIDS-related pneumonia. After his death he was awarded the Presidential Medal of Freedom.

Arthur Ashe did not choose how or when he would end his life's journey. That is not for us to choose. We only have the opportunity to choose success along the way. That happens when we have a clear understanding of our values, a worthwhile vision for our life, and use them to respond meaningfully to the challenges life hands us. In this way success becomes not a destination at the end of our lives, but a journey we live and enjoy each day. In his last years, Arthur Ashe did have the opportunity to write a memoir. The title he chose speaks volumes about his attitude toward his journey, filled with both triumph and adversity. He titled the memoir *Days of Grace*.

My own personal life has had many twists, turns, and setbacks, which I could not have predicted. They have included the breakup of a partnership, being diagnosed with cancer, the divorce of a daughter, and worst of all, the untimely death of my 39-year-old daughter. At the time, I perceived each of these events as the worst possible thing that had ever happened to me. Over time, through faith, prayer, and the conscious choice to look for the positive in each of these experiences, they became my greatest teachers and stepping stones to new levels of maturity and growth.

Each of our lives is a unique story with many twists and turns. I have come to believe that it is not what happens to us that matters, it is how we respond to it that matters most. Choose to look for the positive in every adversity and always remember that the journey of success is never a straight line.

[i] *The Game: My 40 Years in Tennis*, Jack Kramer, 1979

## Chapter Five Recap

## Setting Goals: How will you get from here to there?

1. **Writing down** goals has a measurable, positive impact on their achievement. Write down your goals to crystallize your thinking and provide accountability, then track your progress.

2. Make your goals **S.M.A.R.T.** – Specific, Measurable, Attainable, Realistic, and Tangible.

3. Break down long range goals into shorter term goals and manageable action steps.

4. Life has many twists and turns; it is not what happens to us that matters most, but **how we respond** to it.

SEVEN STEPS TO A LIFE OF SIGNIFICANCE

## Chapter Six

"20 percent of focused effort results in 80 percent outcome of results!"
– *Vilfredo Pareto*

# HIGH PAYOFF ACTIVITIES: How Can You Maximize Your Effectiveness?

**Part One: The Pareto Principle and High Payoff Activities**
As you seek to live a life of significance based on your values and vision, you may find yourself challenged by the need to get more done in less time. You have your mission clearly in view, and in order to progressively accomplish it, you need to maximize the potential of your limited time and energy.

A simple formula handed down to us by an economist and political scientist, Vilfredo Pareto, can help you focus on being more effective and efficient. Pareto noticed that in his garden at home, 80% of the peas came from 20% of the pea pods. This simple observation, repeated in the economic sphere, became known as the 80/20 rule, or the Pareto Principle. It states that roughly 80% of effects come from 20% of causes.

In your career, that means that 80% of your results come from 20% of your activities. In business, 80% of your sales come from 20% of your clients. In your personal life as well, 80% of your results come from 20% of the things you do.

The inverse is also true. 80% of the things you do give you only 20% of your results. It means that in business 80% of your clients give you only 20% of your sales. It also means that 80% of your sales typically come from 20% of your products. It may be more difficult to accept (and yet every bit as important) that 80% of the things you do in your personal life give you only 20% of your results. That means we spend the majority of our time working in ways that are minimally productive!

William Curtis, MD., of Corpus Christi, Texas, applies the Pareto Principle in his medical practice. He works with his patients to make lifestyle changes knowing that 20% of the things we do give us 80% of our results. He focuses on simple things people can do that will give the greatest results (for example, limiting alcohol consumption or doing some type of exercise three times a week). These simple steps that represent only 20% of what we do for our health actually give us 80% of our results, making them the most important. If you focus on the most important things that give the greatest benefit, you can achieve more with your finite resources of time and energy.

Some musicians are using the Pareto Principle to maximize their practice time. They identify the 20% of practice activities and techniques that give them 80% of their results, and focus on those. Athletes are using the 80/20 rule, recognizing that out of ten training routines they do, there are two that are most essential to their sport. By focusing more of their time on the most beneficial routines, they maximize the value of their training. Marketing experts know that 80% of their results come from 20% of their advertising; they then identify and leverage their most powerful marketing tools.

My time and energy are precious. I value the life that has been given to me, and I want to make the most of it. If you do, too, then I challenge you to look at every area of your life through the lens of the Pareto Principle. Identify which activities make up the 20% that give you 80% of your results, and make a plan to focus more on those. These are your "high-payoff activities."

Conversely, identify the activities that are currently taking up 80% of your time and energy, but only giving you 20% of your results. Cut back on those – they are your "low-payoff activities."

They are the activities you can target for eliminating, delegating, simplifying, or automating. A "stop doing" list is as important as a "to do" list. Start using the 80/20 rule today to maximize your results as you work to realize your vision of a life of true significance!

## Part Two: Using High Payoff Activities to Multiply Your Effectiveness

Now that you understand the Pareto Principle, you know that 20% of your activities are the key to obtaining 80% of your results. These are the most important things you do. Identifying them clearly is crucial to your success in each area of life.

I recommend that everyone's list of high-payoff activities begin with planning, and we'll discuss that in more detail later. In my experience careful planning for the execution of SMART (specific, measurable, attainable, realistic and tangible) goals is the most powerful productivity tool of all. Planning for the achievement of pre-determined personal goals keeps you focused on what matters most.

I also suggest that one of your high-payoff activities be personal and professional development. Steven Covey calls it "sharpening the saw," and it is the pinnacle of his "Seven Habits." I've been a student of personal and professional development for more than forty years, and I continue to read voraciously on the subject and to implement new ideas for growth. In life, there is no standing still; you either move forward or you fall behind.

Whether through professional development programs like those we offer at Leadership Dynamics, Inc., reading self-improvement books or publications relevant to your industry, or taking courses to sharpen your skills and acquire new ones, the goal is to always keep growing and improving.

If you include planning and personal and professional development on your list of six high-payoff activities at work, that leaves you four more to identify. To determine what those are, write down all the activities you typically do in a given day, and ask the following questions:

- Which of these are the key functions I was hired to do?

- Which of these consistently yields the highest payoff? Think in terms of how much the activity contributes to increasing revenues, raising profitability, lowering costs, or improving customer satisfaction.

- Which of these are the best use of my unique talents and abilities?

When you have answered those questions, your high-payoff activities should come clearly into view. The next step (unless you are self-employed) is to schedule time with your manager to discuss whether, in his view, these are your most important activities. Limit the list to a few key activities. For example, a sales manager might choose training and coaching new hires, referral prospecting, reviewing and analyzing sales reports, and optimizing the use of CRM (customer relationship management) software.

Remember, these activities typically take 20% of your time but yield 80% of your results. The next step, then, is to determine how much time you currently spend in these activities and work to increase that by scheduling more time in each of them. This maximizes your productivity by making the best use of your time and energy.

Why don't people spend more time in their high-payoff activities? Often they don't know what they are! Those who do know are pulled aside by other activities that seem urgent at the moment but are far less productive. In order to spend more time in your high-payoff activities, it is important to also identify those things you are currently doing that are low-payoff activities.

Are you getting side-tracked with other people's priorities? Do you waste time on trivial activities? Are you doing things below your pay scale that could be delegated to others?

Are you producing reports no one reads, making cold calls that yield next to no sales, or spending hours in poorly run, unproductive meetings?

These are the kind of activities that waste people's time. Find your low-payoff activities, do all you can to minimize them. If the activity is truly unproductive, eliminate it. If it is something that someone else can do better or at a lower pay scale, delegate it. Many routine tasks can now be automated, and if none of those are options, work as much as possible to simplify them.

Take the time you have saved by minimizing low-payoff activities and invest in your high-payoff activities, then watch your productivity—and morale—soar!

The concept of high-payoff activities also applies to your personal life. When it comes time to relax and revitalize, for example, there are clearly some activities that are more effective than others!

Identify the things in each area of your personal life that yield the highest benefits.

Take note of the things you do that take up a lot of time, but aren't really that beneficial. What kind of results might you get if you traded half an hour of TV time for a brisk walk outdoors? Would a board game or shooting some hoops with the kids create a more positive impact than doing that extra bit of work you brought home?

How different would you feel if you picked up a really good book for twenty minutes instead of spending that time on social media?

The bottom line is this: what are the activities you can do today—and every day—that will most effectively lead you to the life of significance you have envisioned for yourself and your family?

## Chapter Six Recap

# HIGH PAYOFF ACTIVITIES:
## How can you maximize your effectiveness?

1. Use the **80/20 rule** to identify and focus on the activities that give you the highest payoff, and to identify and minimize or eliminate low-payoff activities.

2. The 80/20 rule applies to all areas of life and can help maximize your effectiveness in each.

3. Identify your five **highest payoff work activities**, the key functions you were hired to do and are the best use of your unique talents and abilities. Work to increase the time you spend in these each day.

## Chapter Seven

"We all have dreams. But in order to make dreams come into reality it takes an awful lot of determination, dedication, self-discipline, and effort."
— Jesse Owens

# SELF-DISCIPLINE: Do You Have What it Takes?

**Part One: Personal Responsibility – It's Your Life**

A woman walks into work ten minutes late. In her hand is a cup of coffee from the donut shop. "That woman behind the counter!" she fumes. "She was so slow today!" To hear her, it's not her fault she was late; it was the fault of the woman behind the counter.

A man complains, "There are five places in this town where I'm no longer welcome. Some people just don't know how to forgive and forget." It's not his alcoholism or bad behavior that's to blame; it's that people are unforgiving.

"Business has been bad this past year," people tell me. "I'd like to grow the business, but it isn't happening in this economy." In their mind, their lack of growth isn't about their attitudes or performance, their strategic planning or lack of it; it's the economy.

These are real-life examples of people who aren't taking full responsibility for their lives and their results. When things don't go as they had hoped, they look around to find someone else to blame. If they are in debt, it is their employer's fault. If they are overweight, it's in their genes. If they get a bad grade, it's the teacher's fault. They are experts at the blame game.

Responsibility isn't about finding someone to blame. It's about deciding who is going to do something to make the situation better. You can see the decisions other people make and the circumstances of your life as the source of the problems holding you back, or as the starting gate for the race you will run. You can wallow in your own shortcomings and the mistakes of the past or you forgive yourself and focus on using your strengths to move forward to the life you want.

In 1972, Don Bennett was in a boating accident and lost his right leg. Four months later, he was out on the snow-covered slopes downhill skiing. He had been a jogger before the accident, but now he took up kayaking and canoeing instead. In 1982, he set an outrageous goal: to climb Mt. Rainier in Washington State, one of this country's most difficult peaks. He called the adventure "Hop to the Top," and had crutches custom-made with spikes for mountain climbing. He became the first amputee to make the arduous climb to the peak of that 14,410 foot mountain. His remarkable accomplishment was picked up widely by the media, including an appearance on *Good Morning America*.

Making history was only the beginning for Don Bennett. Three years later he founded the world's first soccer league for amputees, helping others once again enjoy the sport they loved. He became a ski instructor at the Greater Seattle Ski School. He competed nationally in handicapped sports competitions and won a gold and silver medal. Bennett continued to ski "just for the fun of it" after he retired from competitive sports in 1996.[11]

To many people, losing a limb would have been excuse enough to give up sports and an active lifestyle, but not for Don Bennett. He used his circumstances as the context for the new and challenging life he envisioned.

Robert Schuller famously said, "If it's going to be, it's up to me." That summed up his philosophy of taking personal responsibility. Through the unexpected difficulties of my life I have learned a hard lesson: I cannot control everything that happens to me. My conviction, however, is that I can control my own attitudes and behaviors, and that in so doing, I can vastly improve my outcomes.

Life has tested that premise, and I have always found it to be true.

Take an inventory of each area of your life. Look as objectively as you can at your results. Make no excuses, lay no blame. Ask only this: what can I do to go from where I am now to where I want to be? You don't have to do it on your own—no one ever does—but you are the only person on earth who can take responsibility for your life. From this day forward, when you are tempted to make any excuse, bite your tongue and determine instead to do whatever it takes to be the person you hope to be and live the life you have envisioned.

**Part Two: Accountability – Your Commitments to Yourself and Others**
When someone tells me they want to improve their golf game, I ask them how they typically score, and they can always tell me. So can tennis players, baseball players, or anyone else who plays sports seriously. They know where they stand, so it is easy to set a goal to move forward. In business, however, many people don't know how they, or the people who work for them, are actually performing. Why?

While athletes keep score, people in business don't always keep track of the metrics that matter most to their success. They're not sure where they are, so it is difficult to set a goal to move forward. In order to achieve your goals, you need to know where you stand now and then track your progress.

Many people resist tracking because they don't want to be held accountable. They don't realize what a positive force accountability can be! The following steps are part of our tried-and-true goal-setting process at Leadership Dynamics:

1. Write down your goal.

2. Write down all of the benefits to be gained and losses to be avoided by achieving your goal.

3. Write down any obstacles you might encounter and how you will overcome them.

4. Set concrete actions steps that will lead toward the achievement of the goal.

5. Share your goal with a supportive friend or mentor.

6. Track both your action steps and your results.

7. Send regular reports to your friend or mentor, and see what a great difference it makes in achieving your goal!

When Dr. Gail Matthews of Dominican University set out to study the impact of written goals, she expected to find a positive effect on productivity. She found not only empirical evidence that written goals make a difference, but that sharing your goals with a supportive friend and making weekly progress reports added 15% more to a person's goals achievement over just writing them down. In other words, accountability matters! It is a very effective tool for achieving what you set out to do.

Consider the impact of a 15% increase in achieving your goals. What would that look like at work? What could it do for you in your personal life? How much more could you do of what matters most to you if you were 15% more effective? The Gail Matthews study confirms my experience with hundreds of clients that you can do this by sharing your written goals with others who are supportive and letting them hold you accountable on regular basis.

I use a 1-31 day tracking form to hold myself accountable to do the things that mean most to me. These are the behaviors that give me the satisfaction of knowing I am winning each day. I use thermometer graphs to track my action steps toward my most important goals. To track results—revenues, profits, etc.—I use XY graphs. Each XY graph starts with a goal line running from where I am now to where I want to be; then I fill in the actual numbers until I reach the goal. That way I always know if I am on track.

Why would you want to know if you are on track? So that you can make the necessary adjustments along the way to ensure that you end up where you want to be. So that you know where you are, and what it will take to get you to the next level. So that you can have the confidence and joy of seeing your progress toward the life of significance you have envisioned for yourself!

**Part Three: The Discipline of Planning**
"The noble make noble plans, and by noble deeds they stand." (Isaiah 32:8) NIV

You may have heard it said that every hour of planning saves ten hours in execution. That is a pretty bold statement! It is backed up by an old industry observation called the 1:10:100 rule. The 1:10:100 rule says that if a problem is not resolved in the planning stage, it will cost ten times more to fix in the building or testing stage, and one hundred times more to fix in the production stage.

By that measure, spending time in careful and effective planning gives you your best possible return on investment!

For me, regular, systematic planning is a discipline that has become automatic and reflexive. I have a planning affirmation, "3-1-30," meaning that I spend three hours planning each month, one hour planning each week, and twenty to thirty minutes organizing my day. I draw my monthly goals from my quarterly plan, and base my quarterly plan on my one-year goals. My one-year goals reflect my three- and five-year goals, which are based, in turn, on my mission and vision. I call it my Cascading Goals System. It allows me to make the connection between my vision, my long-range goals, and my daily activities.

Proverbs 16:9 says, "In their hearts humans plan their course, but the LORD establishes their steps." In my life I have certainly seen how our plans may have to be put on hold by life-changing events. Some of these events have inspired me to see life's priorities differently and adjust my goals accordingly. We plan with humility and it would be foolhardy to carve our plans in stone. Life is not like that. I would still rather see my best-laid plans sometimes go awry than live aimlessly without a plan at all!

Planning gives us the hope and means of bringing to fruition our noblest aspirations. The French writer Antoine de Saint-Exupery said, "A goal without a plan is just a wish."

Planning takes our desires and gives them a track to run on. Without planning you run the risk that your vision will be only imagination, your mission an unfulfilled dream, and your goals merely thoughts on paper. Planning lays the groundwork for what Paul J. Meyer called "the progressive realization of worthwhile, predetermined, personal goals" – a definition of success I embrace.

By this time in our process you have established a vision of the life you want to live. That is the "why" of what you do, who you really are, and the meaning and purpose behind it all. You have identified the mission that answers "how" you will make that vision a reality. You have identified long and short-term goals that are "what" you will do to fulfill your mission. Planning breaks down the larger goals into manageable steps and answers any remaining questions, identified during the goal-setting process, including:

> 1. What are the specific actions steps required to reach the next step in each goal?

2. What target dates will you set for the accomplishment of each action step, and when will you schedule the time to do them?

3. Whose help will you need, and who needs to know about your goals?

4. How will you track progress toward your goal?

These are all vital questions in the planning process, and part of the discipline of planning is investing the right amount of time and effort into each one. Breaking down the goal into action steps allows you to see just what needs to be done, to order the steps in logical sequence, and to identify the amount of time needed for each. Identifying obstacles helps you see them ahead of time and find the resources and solutions to overcome them. Setting target dates is a great way to motivate yourself and build in accountability.

Keep in mind that you won't be able to "make time" for your action steps – you'll have to schedule the time. Block out specific times on your calendar to work on action steps, and respect them as you would any other appointment. Plan ahead to involve others who are important to your success. You may need buy-in, cooperation, logistical support, funding, or even advice. The sooner you let people know how they can help you, the better your chances of getting what you need. Finally, tracking your progress helps ensure that you stay on track and accomplish your goal in the allotted time.

I believe planning is the guardian of all the other disciplines. Paul J. Meyer, a pioneer in personal and corporate development and my greatest mentor, said, "Productivity is never an accident. It is always the result of a commitment to excellence, intelligent planning, and focused effort." Schedule time today to begin planning for the achievement of what matters most to you!

## Part Four: Affirmations – The Discipline of Positive Self-Talk

We all have a constant stream of thought running through our minds. If you have ever tried quieting your mind in prayer or meditation, you know how difficult it is *not* to think. These thoughts amount to hundreds of words per minute, about all kinds of things. Many of these thoughts are based on our past conditioning. We tell ourselves what we can or can't do, and what we should or shouldn't do. We make predictions about what will happen next, or comment internally about what is happening now. Some of our self-talk is positive, but much is negative, for example:

> "I knew this would happen; it always does."

> "He's doing it again; nothing ever changes."

> "This is crazy. We're getting nowhere."

> "I just can't do this. I'm no good at it."

Do you recognize these thoughts? When you focus on them, what impact do they have on you? Negative self-talk is a reality for most people, and it reduces motivation and performance. It also robs us of the joy and enthusiasm we could be experiencing moment by moment.

The answer isn't to deny your feelings. They are real and valid, and acknowledging them in the moment is healthy. Being mindful of your feelings helps you see them with greater objectivity. When you do that, you can process them more readily.

As we process our feelings, we can also change our self-talk. Through a little disciplined effort, we can transform our internal monologue so that it raises our confidence, creates a positive outlook, and helps move us toward the accomplishment of what matters most to us.

We can recondition our own minds, leaving behind negative, limiting beliefs about ourselves and replacing them with thoughts that align with our vision and our values. Because our behaviors are based on our attitudes and beliefs about ourselves and others, when we change our thinking, we change our performance.

Of course, a person who suffers from low self-esteem, depression, or other mental health issues cannot simply talk themselves into being well any more than self-talk alone could cure a common cold. On the road to recovery with qualified professional help, however, mindfulness of our feelings and adjusting our inner monologue can be powerful tools. Affirmations are a useful way of shifting our focus from self-defeating thoughts to empowering, positive ones.

Affirmations are statements that support the changes you want to make in your life. Used consistently over time, they can help re-train your brain to respond in ways that support your goals. There are three characteristics of a powerful affirmation. They are:

1. First person
2. Present tense
3. Positive

Affirmations are most effective when they are in the first person, that is, they begin with "I." The word "I" triggers the mind to pay attention to the statement that follows. It is about us, our behavior, and our results.

If, for example, I am having difficulty maintaining healthy eating habits, it is more powerful to say, "I support an active lifestyle through healthy choices," than, "People support active lifestyles through healthy choices." An "I" statement stimulates a personal response that supports the choice I want to make. In a group setting, "I" statements are better than "we" statements because I can only control my own choices, not those of others.

Affirmations are most powerful in the present tense. The present tense stimulates the mind to respond as though the statement were true. It does this by creating what psychologists call "cognitive dissonance," an internal conflict between what we are saying and what we know is currently true.

For instance, if you wake up feeling poorly rested and dreading the day ahead, but choose to say to yourself, "I have abundant energy and face each day with enthusiasm," you set up cognitive dissonance. Our minds do not like cognitive dissonance, and will seek to resolve the conflict. A strong and healthy mind will work to reduce the gap between the message and reality by raising our behavior and feelings to the level of the affirmation.

An affirmation like the example above is not meant to be a denial or repression of the way you actually feel when you get up in the morning. You know how you feel; you can and should acknowledge that. Now you can make a choice either to focus on the tiredness and dread, or the affirmation of energy and enthusiasm. It is what the French psychologist Emile Coué called "autosuggestion."

By stating in the present tense what you want to be true, you send a powerful signal to your brain. Affirmations can cue our brains to change the way we feel and bring us closer to the desired state.

Affirmations, then, are also most effective when they are positive. Many people, for instance, are terrified of speaking in public. If they are called on to make a speech, they go to the podium saying things like, "I'm so nervous I feel sick. Look at me, I'm shaking. I'm going to forget everything I wanted to say." That only makes them feel and perform worse! It becomes a self-fulfilling prophecy.

On the other hand, if you walk to the podium and repeat to yourself, "I am confident and relaxed speaking before a group," your brain can respond by boosting your confidence and relaxing your body. (Some people mistakenly formulate affirmations in the negative: "When I go up to speak, I will not be afraid." What is the last thing you hear? "Afraid." It triggers the very sensation you don't want, by focusing on it. Keep your affirmations positive.)

When I first went into sales, I was green and not well-prepared to sell to company executives. Through experience I recognized that CEOs can smell fear! I determined to change my mind-set and overcome my fears. I did it with a simple affirmation: "I am fearless." First person, present tense, and positive. I have sold successfully to top executives across many industries, and those three words – "I am fearless" – were of inestimable value to me. I must have repeated those words a thousand times. They reconditioned my brain to respond with confidence and poise in just about any situation I encounter.

You can use affirmations to improve your performance in every area of life. Review the goals you have set in each area. What affirmations would help you overcome your past conditioning and motivate you to succeed in each goal you have set? Here are some examples from the many I have created for the different parts of my life:

1. I have strength for all things through God who empowers me

2. I eat and feed my body nutritious foods, which optimize my health, vitality and mental acuity

3. I practice and maintain an attitude of gratitude

4. I set and work toward the progressive achievement of all my personal, family, and business goals

5. I maintain the discipline of 30 hours of exercise per month to ensure my health, energy, and fitness

6. I look for and find the positive in all circumstances

There is no question, moving forward, about whether you will use self-talk. We all do every day. The question is whether it will be negative or positive; whether it will undermine or support the life of significance you have envisioned. Start now changing your inner monologue, and harness the power of positive affirmations!

**Part Five: The Discipline of Visualization**
In Chapter Two, I challenged you to create a vision that would lay the foundation for a life of significance. Now, as you embark on that life, I challenge you to clearly visualize what it will be like when you have accomplished your goals. When you reach your five-year financial goal, what will that look like? When you reach your ideal weight, how will that look and feel? When you have accomplished your educational goals this quarter, exactly what will that look like?

Take the vision, mission, and goals you have set and create a crystal clear mental picture of the outcome of each.

In 1987, a young Canadian comic from a poor family dreamed of making it big in Hollywood. He created a powerful visualization of what it would be like to be a successful film comedian. It was a check, written to himself, for $10 million "for acting services rendered." The date on the check was November of 1995. By 1994 he had reportedly received $10 million for his role in (ironically) "Dumb and Dumber." By 1995, this comedian, Jim Carrey, was asking $20 million per film and was Hollywood's hottest comedy star. Not so dumb!

Having a clear vision is smart; creating and using powerful visualizations is smarter still. Many top athletes, including Jack Nicklaus and Mohammed Ali, have used the practice of visualization to drive their success. Studies now show that a detailed mental workout (going through the motions in your mind) activates the same areas of the brain that a physical workout does. When you imagine something vividly, you stimulate and strengthen the same neural pathways used in actual performance. Your brain responds accordingly, including building muscle strength, muscle memory, and motor skills.

A recent study at the University of Chicago, for instance, demonstrated that people who only spent time visualizing themselves making free throws one hour a day improved by nearly as much as those who actually practiced free throwing for the same amount of time. There is now ample evidence that visualization can enhance both sports performance and motivation.

Many musicians use the same techniques to improve their skills and performance. They visualize themselves singing or playing through a piece at times and in places where they cannot actually practice. Actors like Will Smith have used visualization both to overcome personal hardship and to create more authentic characters on stage and in film.

You too can use visualization to achieve the things that are most significant to you.

Here's how. First, identify your top six goals, preferably one from each area of life (Physical, Mental, Family, Spiritual, Social, and Financial and Career). Using your senses, imagine vividly what it will be like when you achieve each goal. How will you feel? Where will you be? What will the surroundings look like? What will you hear? Attach a stimulating and pleasurable sensory experience and a positive feeling to every goal. For instance:

- I have completed my sales goal and deposited the commission check. I am feeling a great sense of accomplishment while relaxing and celebrating with a week in St. Croix, feeling the sun on my skin, hearing the waves on the beach, smelling the salt air, and seeing the sparkling light on the water...

- I have finished my Master's degree and I am feeling elated as I walk to the front of the hall to receive my diploma, hearing the applause of the audience, seeing my family looking on proudly, and feeling that parchment in my hand at last...

- I have reached my goal weight and am thrilled to be buying new clothes in my ideal size, feeling the perfect fit, happy with my reflection in the mirror, filled with energy and confidence…

- I have achieved my goal to raise $3,000 to sponsor a well in a developing country. I can see the looks of joy on the faces of children as they drink and wash, and hear the happy shouts of women who will no longer have to carry water for miles every day, and I know that my life has significance for me and for others.

When you have a compelling mental picture for each goal, create a physical visualization as well. You can make a separate collage for each goal, using photo editing software, creative scrapbooking techniques, or simple cut-and-paste. You can also create a vision board for your home, where you collect pictures related to the accomplishment of your goals. Keep these where you will see them every day, and let them inspire and motivate you.

Finally, schedule a time each day to review your goals, recite your affirmations, and practice your visualizations. Develop the discipline of picturing the achievement of your goals daily. Start now and harness the proven power of visualization!

"Whatever you vividly imagine, ardently desire, sincerely believe, and enthusiastically act upon must inevitably come to pass." Paul J. Meyer

## Chapter Seven Recap

## SELF-DISCIPLINE: Do you have what it takes?

1. You alone can take **responsibility** for your life; you alone can choose to do what it takes to achieve the life you envision.

2. **Track progress** toward your goals using graphs and charts. **Share** your written goals and regular progress reports with a supportive friend.

3. Develop the habit of regular, systematic **planning**: long term, yearly, quarterly, monthly, weekly and daily.

4. Use **affirmations** – positive self-talk – to support the changes you want to make and the goals you want to achieve.

5. Create a compelling mental picture for goals in each area of life, and post **visualizations** where you can see them every day.

6. **Review** your goals, affirmations, and visualizations every day.

# Final Thoughts

My life experience has tested and validated the beliefs in this book. I also believe that "It is no use walking anywhere to preach unless our walking is our preaching." (St. Francis) I practice the attitudes, behaviors, and skill sets I have outlined on a daily basis.

By now, most of them are habits. I have become competent at these disciplines through *progressive* daily practice and by creating rituals and routines. As a result, I do these things without even thinking, automatically and reflexively. As an early riser, I am able to accomplish most of the things that matter most to me before 9:00 a.m.

I believe that by following the process outlined in this book, you too can adopt the strategies and habits that lead to a life of significance. I truly have a reverence for our human potential. I believe each of us has been gifted in ways that make us unique and capable of making significant contributions to our families, communities, workplaces, and the world. I have come to believe that human beings possess three basic spheres of potential. They are the physical, mental, and spiritual dimensions. Each area is important on its own, but when combined together, their impact multiplies exponentially.

My life's journey has been an exploration of these areas of human potential. As a young man, my primary focus was on my physical potential. I overcame the self-image and self-esteem issues that came with being a scrawny kid. Step by step, I developed my physical strength and athletic ability. New doors of opportunity opened for me. However, as my horizons expanded, I came to understand that no matter how strong I thought I was my physical potential was limited.

As I think back on that stage of my development, I realize that my primary focus was more on myself than others. My potential for significance was also limited. I began to explore other areas of growth as a human being.

The next area I chose to explore was the potential of my mind. My motivation came from attending a seminar given by Jim Rohn. Jim said, "Those who do not read are no better off than those who cannot." He also said that anyone who reads a book a month would be able to double their income in one year! That day I established a goal of reading twelve books in the next year and to double my income. I accomplished both goals.

The ability to create value for others and myself through the development of my mind fascinated me. I became a student of personal development. I increased my reading goal from 12 to 24 books in the next year. I set another goal to attend a minimum of four personal development seminars during the year.

I developed the affirmation "I read and study a minimum of one hour per day to learn and apply new ideas that increase my knowledge and my ability to add value to all of my personal and professional relationships." My career began to fast track. At 28 years old, I was offered a partnership in the business where I worked and became president of one of its divisions.

I increased my reading goal to a minimum of 50 books per year and learned that my mental potential was exponentially greater than my physical potential. The habit of reading and learning became the source of many opportunities and blessings for me.

It was the catalyst for developing the knowledge and experience which allowed me to found and grow two successful businesses of my own.

Leadership Dynamics, Inc. was the vehicle for me to turn my avocation of personal development into a meaningful vocation. It has provided me with a platform to contribute value to many individuals and companies.

The tangible and intangible rewards have been great. Most importantly, the development of my mental potential allowed me to move in the direction of greater outward focus, contribution, and towards a life of greater significance.

As is the case with all of us, life has presented its challenges along the way. Family health crises, the deaths of cherished family members, the loss of beloved mentors and friends, accidents, business challenges, and various disappointments were among them. Starting out as a young couple, my wife and I had to face and overcome many trials. The life skills that we developed as a result of overcoming them increased our capacity to handle life's struggles and become more resilient.

In April of 2007 I was diagnosed with cancer. Some of you know what a life-altering experience being diagnosed with cancer can be for both you and your family. My initial response was to ask "why me?" I rationalized that since I was a good person and lived a healthy lifestyle, I did not deserve this fate. Nothing that I ever faced in business was ever a life-or-death situation. Taking on a fight with cancer was just that, and it had my full attention.

My cancer diagnosis was a significant turning point for me. I applied all the disciplines I had developed in the physical and mental dimensions of my life. I increased my physical exercise from 30 to 40 hours a month to improve my endurance and prepare my body for what was to come.

I set a goal to study, research treatment options, and to qualify specialists. I spent countless hours gathering information that would allow my family and me to make an intelligent and informed decision about how we would choose to wage this war against cancer.

In the middle of all of this, I came to realize how little control most of us actually have over many of the things that happen to us. I felt a need to identify and tap into a power greater than my own physical and mental abilities. I had often prayed before, but now I developed the discipline of daily prayer and meditation. I learned how to quiet my mind, shut out the outside world, and to be present to the moment.

My prayers changed from only talking to God to listening to God, and I began to experience greater peace, tranquility, and insight. I began to sense a warm and loving presence during these times which gave me great comfort. My fear and anxiety began to dissipate and I developed a sense of well-being. I began to trust that through God's grace I would return to perfect health.

At the same time, I continued the physical and mental disciplines I had developed. These were the things I could control and for which I could take personal responsibility. I let go of the things I could not control and turned them over to the higher power of God. This experience helped me discover and tap into the potential of my spiritual dimension.

In July of 2007 I entered the Lahey Clinic for surgery. I had the very best care and the most advanced procedures available. The operation and my recovery were very successful. As of this writing I have been cancer free for 7.5 years. When I combined my spiritual potential with my physical and mental dimensions, I discovered a synergy that increased my capacity exponentially.

Looking back, I realize that the discovery and development of my spiritual potential through all of life's challenges was a blessing in disguise designed to prepare me for greater ones to come. One year later, we lost my father to Alzheimer's disease. Before I even had time to fully grieve his passing, tragedy struck our family again. The morning after we buried my father, our beloved 39 year-old daughter, Liisa, died in her sleep, leaving her husband and five young children behind. The period that followed was one of the darkest and most challenging times that my family has experienced.

One week after burying Liisa in Richmond, VA, we returned home to Massachusetts. The first day after our return I resumed my daily discipline of prayer and meditation. That day, I had a strong urge to open my Bible. It opened to the 23$^{rd}$ Psalm, which I read slowly and prayerfully. I read the words:

> "Even though I walk through a dark valley, I fear no harm for you are at my side; your rod and staff give me courage."[1]

As I reflected on these words, I realized that this dark cloud of grief was the valley of darkness described in this psalm. I realized that in order to continue life after the loss of a child, it was necessary not to get stuck in the valley, but to walk through the valley.

You never get over the loss of a child, but you must learn to live with it through the grace of God. My wife, Lois, and I made a conscious choice to hold each other's hands and walk through this dark valley together. After almost seven years, I can say that there can be light, hope and joy again, despite experiencing the valley of darkness. We found it by sharing in the lives of our grandchildren, and through reaching out to others who have also experienced loss.

We have experienced it in performing small acts of kindness for others and doing our best to bring light, joy, and hope to them, and also in the small acts of kindness that others have bestowed upon us in our times of need.

Every one of us has a story to tell. We all experience unique challenges and turning points in our lives. My story is no more noteworthy than anyone else's ... it is simply my story. What I have learned is that, in the words of Epictetus, "It is not what happens to you, but how you react to it that matters."

If you are able to fully appreciate and apply the ideas that I have shared with you in this book, you will be able to tap into your physical, mental, and spiritual potential to manage the challenges that life inevitably brings to each of us. More importantly, you will be able to turn the setbacks and obstacles of life into experiences that develop your perseverance, character and your ability to optimize your potential and capacity to add value to others.

When you do this your focus changes from being the best *in* the world to being the best *for* the world. It is then that you begin to live a life of significance. That is my wish and hope for you.

---

[1] Psalm 23:4, Saint Joseph Edition - New American Bible

# About the Co-Authors

## *Kevin Patterson*

Kevin Patterson worked as a journalist, teacher, and human rights advocate in Jerusalem and Bethlehem. He is an ordained minister, and has been pastor of the First Baptist Church of West Townsend, Massachusetts since 1994.

In 2001 he joined the team at Leadership Dynamics, Inc., working to bring clients to their next level of personal and professional development.

## *Leslie Brown Scales*

Leslie Brown Scales is the Director of Business Development, facilitator and professional coach at Leadership Dynamics, Inc. Leslie also serves as President of The International Leadership Institute for Women, a strategic personal and organizational development company specializing in helping women become the best versions of themselves.

She graduated from Babson College with a degree in Entrepreneurial Studies, specializing in Marketing and Management. She is a frequent speaker to audiences delivering dynamic addresses on the topics of Women's Leadership, Personal Development and Goal Setting. Her greatest personal successes are her two beautiful children, Olivia and Bailey.

# FOOTNOTES

[1] Frankl, Viktor E., *Man's Search for Meaning*, Washington Square Press, Simon and Schuster, New York, 1963, p. 104.).
[2] Attitude is Everything, by Francie Baltazar-Schwartz.
Study carried out by Professor Kay-Tee Khaw of the Clinical Gerontology Unit of Cambridge University's [3] School of Clinical Medicine at Addenbrooke's Hospital.
[4] Becca Levy, assistant professor in the Department of Epidemiology and Public Health at Yale, et al., published in the Journal of Personality and Social Psychology, August 2002.
[5] Lynne C Giles, et al., in the British Medical Association's Journal of Epidemiology and Community Health. Jul 2005; 59: 574 - 579.
[6] "Richer, better-educated people live longer than poorer, less-educated people." Angus Deaton of the National Bureau of Economic Research, "Health, Income, and Inequality," NBER Reporter, Spring 2003, p. 9.
[7] The findings are contained in a study conducted jointly by Rick Rogers, of CU-Boulder, Robert Hummer and Christopher Ellison, of the University of Texas at Austin, and Charles Nam, from Florida State University, and published in Living and Dying in the USA: Behavioral, Health, and Social Differentials of Adult Mortality, Richard G. Rogers, et al., London, Academic Press, 2000, p. 101.
[8] Shan Tsai, et al. Brit Med J 01/21/05.
[9] "...volunteering has a protective effect on mortality among those who volunteered for one organization or for forty hours or less over the past year." Neal Krause, School of Public Health and Institute of Gerontology University of Michigan, and Benjamin A. Shaw, School of Public Health and Institute of Gerontology University of Michigan, Role-Specific Feelings of Control and Mortality, Psychology and Aging, December 2000 Vol. 15, No. 4, 617-626.
[11] MA Musick, AR Herzog, and JS House Volunteering and mortality among older adults: findings from a national sample, Journals of Gerontology Series B: Psychological Sciences and Social Sciences, Vol. 54, Issue 3 S173-S180.
[12] Plaster, Billie Jean, *He Made Climbing History*, Sandpoint Magazine, Summer 1999.

# NOTES TO SELF

# NOTES TO SELF

# NOTES TO SELF

# NOTES TO SELF

www.LeadershipDynamicsInc.com